1513

B
POL   Lillegard, Dee

           James K. Polk

$17.27

DATE			

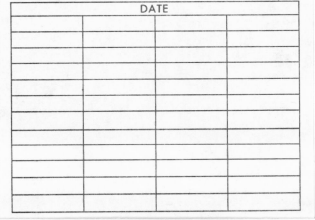

BAKER & TAYLOR BOOKS

JAMES K. POLK

ENCYCLOPEDIA
of PRESIDENTS

James K. Polk

Eleventh President of the United States

By Dee Lillegard

Consultant: Charles Abele, Ph.D.
Social Studies Instructor
Chicago Public School System

ℚP CHILDRENS PRESS ®

CHICAGO

President James K. Polk's home in Columbia, Tennessee

Dedication: For Joyce and Pat, who played Presidents with me.

Library of Congress Cataloging-in-Publication Data

Lillegard, Dee.
   James K. Polk.

   (Encyclopedia of presidents)
   Includes index.
   Summary: A biography of the eleventh American
president, whose term in office saw great expansion
of the western frontier.
   1. Polk, James K. (James Knox), 1795-1849—
Juvenile literature.   2. Presidents—United States—
Biography—Juvenile literature.   [1. Polk, James K.
(James Knox), 1795-1849.   2. Presidents]   I. Title.
II. Series.
E427.L55   1988   973.6'1'0924   [B]   [92]   87-35188
ISBN 0-516-01351-3

Childrens Press®, Chicago
Copyright ©1988 by Regensteiner Publishing Enterprises, Inc.
All rights reserved. Published simultaneously in Canada.
Printed in the United States of America.
   3 4 5 6 7 8 9 10 R 97 96 95 94 93 92 91 90

Picture Acknowledgments

The Bettmann Archive—11 (bottom), 25, 36, 54,
56, 60 (2 pictures), 61 (bottom), 64, 77
(bottom), 78 (2 pictures)

John Carter Brown Library, Brown University—
77 (top)

Historical Pictures Service, Chicago—9, 11 (top),
13, 15, 16, 22, 23, 24, 26, 32, 34, 35, 38, 43, 45
(2 pictures), 51 (bottom), 55(bottom), 62, 66, 69
(2 pictures), 70, 71, 73 (bottom), 75 (top), 80,
82, 87, 89

Courtesy Library of Congress—4, 5, 6, 8, 29, 47,
48, 51 (top), 55 (top), 61 (top), 72, 73 (top), 84,
88

Missouri Historical Society—75 (bottom)

New York Historical Society—74

North Wind Picture Archives—40

Courtesy The Smithsonian Institution—79
(bottom)

Courtesy Travellers' Rest (Overton house)—31

Courtesy U.S. Bureau of Printing and
Engraving—2

Courtesy U.S. Department of the Navy—79 (top)

Cover design and illustration
by Steven Gaston Dobson

James Knox Polk

Table of Contents

James K. Polk

Chapter 1

"Dark Horse"

James Polk would never give up. He knew what he wanted and he wouldn't take no for an answer. Small and slender, Polk carried himself in a dignified manner. His broad forehead, steel gray eyes, and stern expression made him look as determined as he was.

Polk wanted to be vice-president of the United States. In 1840 he was turned down for the Democratic vice-presidential nomination. From 1839 to 1841, Polk served as governor of Tennessee, but he was twice defeated in his bids for a second term. In August 1843, after these three losses, it looked as if his political career were over.

Polk was not alone. The Democrats and the Whigs were the two most important political parties in the United States at the time. Whigs were trouncing Democrats in elections everywhere. Polk was a Democratic party leader, but now his leadership was seriously in question.

It seemed certain that in 1844 former president Martin Van Buren would once again be the Democratic presidential candidate, running against the Whig Henry Clay. Polk wanted to be Van Buren's running mate. But with his string of defeats, how could he hope to be chosen?

Andrew Jackson in his last days

Part of the Democratic party's problem was that many Democrats were fighting among themselves. Not only would Polk have to restore his own position of leadership, but he would have to unite the warring factions of the party. It seemed like an impossible task. But Polk had a very important person behind him.

As a congressman years before, Polk had won the friendship and confidence of Andrew Jackson. The revered military hero, who had been the seventh president of the United States, was now approaching the end of his life. His body wracked by the pain of old battle wounds, Jackson lay suffering at the Hermitage, his home near Nashville, Tennessee. But on September 20, 1843, he wrote to a trusted friend: "Tennessee will support Van Buren, & if Polk is selected for Vice President, he will carry the State most assuredly." Later Jackson repeated this message even more strongly to Van Buren.

Martin Van Buren

Jackson's support was highly encouraging. But Polk had a lot of work to do. First he would have to assert his leadership in Tennessee. He hurried to Nashville, where party leaders from every section of the state were meeting. He coaxed, bargained, and persuaded almost all the important Democratic politicians to support him as the vice-presidential candidate at their next convention. Only the most stubborn could resist him.

Polk also persuaded several of his Democratic friends to write letters to Democrats far and near. These letters urged the Democrats to unite against the Whigs. They warned that if Henry Clay were elected, the federal government would have too much control over the individual states. The country must be saved from Clay's "American System," whereby high tariffs would benefit the North and the federal government would pay for roads and canals throughout the states.

Polk had to win the support of Democratic party leaders and factions in other states as well. This would be much more difficult. Meanwhile, some Democrats were trying to destroy Van Buren's chances for the presidential candidacy. But for a time, it seemed as if Van Buren had won out. In December 1843, a congressman and close friend of Polk's wrote to him: "All the fragments of our party seem likely to unite upon Van Buren [and] make his nomination unanimous. . . ." But now many Democrats came out against Polk as the vice-presidential candidate. Their opposition to Polk was so strong that his defeat seemed certain. He despaired of "the schemes . . . to defeat me." But still he would not give up.

By this time, the annexation of Texas to the United States had become a burning issue. Texas had won its independence from Mexico in 1836, but Mexico still would not recognize this. There was a danger of war with Mexico if the United States annexed Texas. The fact that there was slavery in Texas made the issue even more difficult. Many northerners were against annexing a slave territory.

The Texas question threatened to tear the Democratic party to pieces. Neither presidents Jackson nor Van Buren had wanted to press the issue. In April 1844, a committee of Democrats asked all presidential and vice-presidential candidates to declare their views on Texas. Polk promptly replied that he favored immediate annexation. (Polk also proposed taking the Oregon Territory, thus keeping a balance between slave and free soil.) But Van Buren, like his Whig opponent Clay, came out against Texas annexation. This was a blow to Andrew Jackson.

Above: A pro-annexation demonstration in New Jersey
Below: The Alamo in San Antonio, Texas, scene of a bloody battle

Jackson had helped Van Buren into the presidency in 1836 and had supported him ever since. He knew that, throughout the states, more people were for annexation than against it. A stand in favor of annexation would have given Van Buren a great advantage over Clay. Now, Jackson felt, Van Buren had ruined his own chances for the presidency.

The news of Van Buren's position caused an uproar among the Democrats. Anti-Van Buren circulars were passed around, and the newspapers declared that Van Buren would be a losing candidate. One of Van Buren's supporters abandoned him, saying, "The Breeders of Mules and horses and hogs cry out let us have Texas right or wrong. . . . If those Mexicans come nigh we will eat them up."

Jackson was torn between his friendship with Van Buren and his desire to see Texas annexed to the Union. He hoped the convention could nominate Van Buren but pass a resolution supporting annexation. This might save Van Buren by forcing him to follow the party platform.

A few weeks before the Democratic convention was to be held, Jackson called Polk to the Hermitage. He had made up his mind, and his decision would carry great weight with the Democrats. The party must come up with an entirely new presidential candidate, Jackson declared. Polk later wrote that Jackson said "the candidate for the Presidency should be an annexation man" and that Jackson "openly expresses (what I assure you I had never for a moment contemplated) the opinion that I would be the most available man. . . ."

Presidential candidate Lewis Cass

If Polk had "never for a moment" thought of being the candidate for president, he must have been very surprised at Jackson's words. Nevertheless, not one to show his excitement, he replied simply: "I never aspired so high." Then he added that if Van Buren's name were to be withdrawn, the Democrats could "use my name in any way they may think proper."

Van Buren was not about to withdraw from the race, nor were the other major contenders, Lewis Cass, John C. Calhoun, and James Buchanan. To Polk, the chances for his nomination for the presidency seemed remote. Not even Jackson could make such an unlikely thing happen.

On May 27, 1844, the Democratic convention met in Baltimore, Maryland. According to one delegate, the Baltimore hotels were filled with "the most reckless and desperate system of political intrigue that I have ever witnessed."

The day before the convention began, thunder, lightning, and heavy rains struck. But on the convention floor itself, the political storm was even more violent. Another delegate described such "pulling and hauling" as he had never before seen. At times the chairman could not control the convention.

The fighting was intense. After several days and seven ballots, it was clear to the weary delegates that Van Buren could not be nominated. He needed a two-thirds majority to win the nomination, and too many votes were scattered among the other candidates.

This deadlock could have doomed the Democrats to defeat and destroyed the party. But at this point, the Massachusetts delegate and noted historian George Bancroft proposed James K. Polk as a compromise candidate. On the eighth ballot, Polk received only forty-four delegate votes. But on the ninth ballot, the convention voted overwhelmingly in favor of the man who would become the first "dark-horse" president.

The term "dark horse" was used at the race tracks to refer to a relatively unknown horse. Although Polk was not exactly unknown, he was not exactly famous, either, in the new, growing country that was spreading west. He had won the Democratic presidential nomination. Could he win the presidency?

Henry Clay, statesman and dramatic orator

The compromise seemed like a miracle to the exhausted Democrats. As a final unanimous vote was announced, one man scribbled a note to Polk: "The Convention is shouting. The people in the streets are shouting. The news went to Washington and back by Telegraph whilst the votes were counting and the Congress is shouting. There is one general shout throughout the whole land, and I can't write any more for Shouting. . . ."

It would take yet another "miracle" for James K. Polk to defeat the powerful Henry Clay. At least that's what Clay and the Whigs thought.

Nashville, Tennessee, in the nineteenth century

Chapter 2

Growing Up with Tennessee

James Knox Polk was born around noon on November 2, 1795, in Mecklenburg County, North Carolina. He was the first child of Samuel and Jane Knox Polk and was named after his grandfather James Knox. Grandfather Knox had been a militia captain during the Revolution and was a descendant of John Knox, the founder of Scottish Presbyterianism.

Samuel Polk and his brother Thomas had a double wedding in December 1794, ten weeks after the death of Jane's father. Ezekial Polk gave each of his newly-married sons a 250-acre farm on Little Sugar Creek. James Knox left behind a large estate, including ten slaves, and Jane (or Jenny) received two Negro girls, a feather bed, three cows and calves, a mare, a third of her father's household furniture, and a fifth of his estate. So the young Polks— Sam, age twenty-two, and Jenny, nineteen—got off to a good start. But Baby James—at least from his mother's point of view—was not so fortunate.

Jenny was a strong Presbyterian and wanted her son to be baptized in the Presbyterian church. But on the day of the event, Sam and the local parson quarreled, and the baby was taken home.

James K. Polk would not be baptized until years later when he lay on his deathbed. And then he would choose to die a Methodist, though two Presbyterian ministers stood at his bedside.

The Polk family lived in a log cabin. It was actually two houses with one roof that formed a covered passageway between them. There were mud-chinked chimneys on either end. The cabin looked out over well-cultivated fields that sloped down into a wide bend of Little Sugar Creek. Tobacco, wheat, corn, hemp, peas, barley, and oats were the main crops of this Carolina up-country.

From the Polks' door, the smoke rising from neighboring cabins could be seen. The Great Post Road skirted the slope in front of the cabin and crossed the creek on Samuel Polk's bridge. It was a narrow, rutted road, but every seven days young Jim could watch the carrier of the United States mail pass, northbound one week, southbound the next.

Two miles up the road, Jim's grandfather Ezekial Polk had a plantation, and Charlotte, North Carolina, was only nine miles away. Mecklenburg was a calm, quiet place to live now that the Revolution was over and most of the Indians were gone. Occasionally Jim might see a Catawba Indian on the road, but he would never experience the fierce Indian raids that his Grandfather Polk so vividly recalled.

Jim was a frail child, small for his age. When he was seven, his grandfather Ezekial persuaded most of the Polk clan to move to middle Tennessee. Sam and Jenny refused to go, probably because Jenny did not want to leave her mother and friends.

But more and more people were emigrating westward. Three years later, in 1806, Sam saw greater opportunities for himself in Tennessee. He decided to join his father and the rest of the Polk family.

By now, Jim had two sisters, aged eight and six, and two brothers, one four and the other an infant. There were five more children to come. Except for the baby, the family had to walk with their slaves from Mecklenburg to their new home in Tennessee. Their wagon was heavily loaded, and only when the girls were tired were they allowed to ride in it.

Slowly the group trekked over five hundred miles of mountains and rivers into the valleys of east Tennessee. They passed through Knoxville and walked on over the Cumberland Mountains that isolated middle Tennessee from the eastern part of the state. It took them a month and a half to travel this rough terrain to the fertile Duck River Valley south of Nashville. Here they would live in another log cabin with a stream running behind it.

Sam Polk prospered on the land that Ezekial had set aside for him. But it became increasingly clear that young Jim was not suited to farming. He did his chores dutifully, but his health was poor and he tired quickly. Jim didn't like the pigs or the cows, but he loved horses. He had learned to ride almost as soon as he learned to walk.

Life was not easy for the Polks. They had to produce everything they ate, wore, or otherwise used. Every member of the family was needed to help. As Jim became more and more ill with nauseating stomach pains, he began to lag at his tasks. Worst of all for Jim, he was branded a weakling because he couldn't participate in the rough-and-tumble play of the neighboring farm boys. Alarmed, Sam Polk took his son to see the famous surgeon Doctor Ephraim McDowell in Danville, Kentucky.

It was 1812, and the 230-mile trip on horseback was grueling for Jim. Doctor McDowell diagnosed the problem as gallstones and recommended an operation to have the stones removed.

Weak and wasted, Jim needed several weeks of rest before the operation could be performed. When the time came, he was strapped to a wooden table and held down by McDowell's assistants. They gave him a little brandy to dull the pain, and then the doctor began.

Doctors in those days did not sterilize their instruments. There was a good chance that Jim would die of blood poisoning or bleed to death. But he survived the operation and returned home to display the stones to his family and other admirers. It was an experience he would never forget.

Jim's health improved, but farming was still too hard on him. He was put to work as an apprentice to a merchant in Columbia, about six miles from home. He disliked the confinement and the dull routine, and after a few weeks his father had to bring him home again. But that wasn't what Jim Polk wanted; he wanted to go to school.

Doctor McDowell had written in his diary that Jim Polk was an "uncouth and uneducated" boy. Jim had had no formal education. His parents taught him to read, write, and do arithmetic. They also taught him Thomas Jefferson's ideas about democracy, in which they strongly believed.

In July 1813, seventeen-year-old Jim Polk enrolled in a Presbyterian academy, where he began his classical education. He wrote crudely, spelled poorly, and was older than most of the other students.

Nevertheless, Jim studied with zeal, his health improved, and he was happier than he had ever been when he was younger. Within a year he had made so much progress that his parents sent him to a private school in Murfreesboro, fifty miles northeast of Columbia.

Jim Polk was beginning to develop into a handsome young man, with dark hair and gray eyes. At Murfreesboro he made friends with Anderson Childress, the son of a wealthy merchant. Anderson had a sister, Sarah, who was eleven when Jim first met her. Jim could not have guessed that Sarah would one day be his wife, much less his First Lady.

Young Polk worked hard again at Murfreesboro. He studied not only Greek and Latin, but mathematics, geography, philosophy, astronomy, and literature. He also had the lead part in a class play, proving himself a fair comedian in the role of "Jerry Sneak." By 1815, Jim Polk was considered "the most promising young man in the school." His keen mind thrived on learning, and he was ready to move on to college.

The University of North Carolina at Chapel Hill

At the age of twenty-one, James K. Polk entered the University of North Carolina at Chapel Hill. He had successfully passed the entrance requirements for the second-year class. Polk was courteous and well liked. He was chosen president of the Dialectic Society, which met weekly to debate topics of the day. Many of the debates were over questions that Polk would have to face later. He knew now that he wanted a career in politics, and his participation in the society's debates was excellent preparation.

Steamboats eventually replaced flatboats as river transportation.

In 1818 Polk graduated from the university with highest honors in mathematics and the classics. He had been described as a "correct, punctual, and industrious" student. But he had worked so hard that he was on the verge of collapse and could not immediately set out on the long trip home to Tennessee.

James K. Polk and Tennessee were the same age. The state had been admitted to the Union seven months after Polk was born. Now the look of the raw, undeveloped frontier was gone. There were new towns with fine houses, and steamboats were pushing up Tennessee's rivers.

Nashville attorney Felix Grundy

Sam Polk had moved his family into a two-story brick house on the best street in Columbia. Through land speculation he had come to own thousands of acres of land and more than fifty slaves. This was three decades before the Civil War, which would finally bring slavery to an end.

When Jim reached Columbia, he was anxious to complete preparations to become a lawyer. There were no law schools, so would-be lawyers had to find jobs with established attorneys. They made themselves useful by building fires on chilly mornings, running errands, and writing out copies of important papers. In return, they were allowed to read the attorneys' law books to prepare for the bar examinations.

Jim went to work for the famous Nashville attorney Felix Grundy. He studied hard, and before long other

Sam Houston, soldier and political leader

young attorneys were seeking his legal advice. One of
them was Sam Houston, the Tennessee farm boy who was
destined to be a hero in Texas.

In September 1819, with Grundy's backing, Jim Polk
was elected clerk of the Tennessee state senate. He was in
charge of directing the flow of paperwork. It was a prize
position that paid well—six dollars per day while the
senate was in session. (The senators received only four dollars per day.) This was the beginning of Polk's political
career.

Some of Tennessee's lawmakers were rough, tobacco-
spitting frontiersmen. They slouched back in their seats,
with their boots on their desks and hats on their heads.
Their language was often equally rough. But their debates
taught Polk his first real lessons in politics.

Chapter 3

From Clerk to Congressman

The state legislature rarely met for longer than a month, so Polk was able to finish his law studies. As soon as he passed the bar and became a lawyer, Jim informed his brothers and sisters that, from now on, they could call him James.

Polk's first case was to defend his own father. Sam had lost his temper in an argument with another man. The judge let him off with a one-dollar fine. In return, Sam helped James with the money to build a one-room law office in Columbia and buy a second-hand set of law books.

Tennessee was full of struggling young lawyers. But confusion over land titles gave them all plenty to do. Circuit judges traveled from one county to another, and groups of lawyers rode along on horseback. They stayed overnight at rough county seat taverns, six to a room, and ate together at the long tavern tables. James Polk began to follow the circuit, riding his horse from town to town. He became popular among the traveling lawyers because of his good sense of humor.

Opposite page: Portrait of James Polk

Relaxing together in the evening, these lawyers liked to hear Polk tell amusing stories. He made many friends riding the circuit who would help him in later years.

Polk proved to be a highly successful lawyer. But politics was his real passion. Circuit riding brought him into close contact with the leading men of middle Tennessee. Constant speaking in crowded courtrooms brought him before the voters. And his position as legislative clerk introduced him into the centers of political power. In 1821, Polk sought reelection to the clerkship. He received unanimous support from both factions of the legislature, who could agree on very little else.

Polk developed the reputation of being "a fine fellow." In 1821, his popularity helped him win an election for captain of the local cavalry regiment. Before long he became a major. It seemed that several pretty girls in Columbia wanted to marry him. But none of them interested him for long. Then James Polk renewed his friendship with Anderson Childress, whose sister Sarah had grown up into a very interesting young woman.

Sarah Childress had attended the Female Academy of the Moravians in Salem, North Carolina. There she studied arithmetic, history, and geography—subjects that were not considered "proper" for young ladies. Sarah was also accomplished in music and art and dressed elegantly. James Polk began riding fifty miles from Columbia to Murfreesboro to court her.

Sarah's education and her strong personality had a spurring effect on the ambitious young Polk. He became dissatisfied with the position of clerk and, in 1822,

Opposite page: Sarah Childress, who became James Polk's wife

announced his candidacy for the lower house of the Tennessee legislature. He would have to carry his campaign into the rough frontier, covering far more than the fifty miles to Murfreesboro.

For weeks at a time, Polk rode his horse over the dirt roads from one village to the next. He spoke from tree stumps in every clearing where a few settlers were willing to gather. This sort of "stumping" was the custom of the day. Because Polk was small but a powerful speaker, he came to be called "Napoleon of the Stump" after Napoleon Bonaparte, the small but powerful French hero.

Polk rode long distances between farms to win the support of neighborhood leaders by talking to them and shaking their hands. He ate on the run and slept when and where he could. He was in the saddle for hours at a time in unbearable heat or sloshing through mud in pouring rains.

There was nothing secret about the election. At the polling places, each man who was allowed to vote walked up to a table and declared his choice aloud. As his vote was cast, the voter was cheered or booed by the crowd. Newly arriving voters were sometimes taken by the arm and led aside for last-minute "advice," and fist fights often broke out.

Polk eventually won his seat in the Tennessee legislature by a healthy margin. Now he had a major decision to make. For years the state had been under the control of a faction headed by the wealthiest man in Tennessee, John Overton. But the people rebelled against the special interests Overton represented and elected William Carroll to be governor. Carroll was strongly supported by farmers and laborers.

Judge John Overton

The Overton group expected Polk to support them. After all, Polk's father was a landowner and a director of one of Overton's banks. But James Polk had been elected by farmers and laborers. They reminded him of his Grandfather Ezekial and of his own childhood. He took a stand in favor of Governor Carroll, and in his first term he became the leader of the Carroll forces.

**Felix Grundy
at his desk**

There were heated debates between the two factions. Polk found himself battling Felix Grundy, who was with Overton's group. The man who had helped him become a lawyer was now his opponent. Another famous Tennesseean, Davy Crockett, was on Polk's side. The two legislators battled their foes together. But Polk had a mind of his own. In the long run, he would not be the pawn of any group. It was General Andrew Jackson who unwittingly put him to the test.

At this time, the United States had no national conventions to nominate candidates for president. State legislatures passed resolutions naming the candidates they favored, but Congress made the nominations. When Jackson declared his bid for the presidency, Grundy and the Overton men backed him for senator, hoping to regain their own power through Jackson's popularity. Governor Carroll selected another candidate to oppose Jackson.

Polk was against the Overton people, who backed Jackson, but was strongly in favor of Jackson himself. However, if he threw his support to Jackson, he would have to go against Governor Carroll. As a leader of Carroll's group, Polk could win Jackson the votes he needed to become senator and then, perhaps, president. But if Jackson lost, Polk could lose right along with him.

Polk made a difficult decision that would influence the rest of his career. He took a stand for Andrew Jackson. Davy Crockett and most of the Carroll people stood by their own candidate. But there were enough who followed Polk to win Jackson a place in the Senate and save his chance for the presidency. Jackson never forgot that Polk went against his own people to back him.

For James Polk, the choice of a wife was much easier. On New Year's Day, 1824, he and Sarah were married. A large country wedding was held at the Childress plantation house near Murfreesboro. One of the guests commented in a letter that Sarah was not strikingly beautiful, but that she was witty and graceful and "an intelligent and animated conversationalist." Another guest noted that "her eyes looked as if she had a great deal of spice."

Davy Crockett, frontiersman and politician

Sarah saw little of her husband for the first two years of their marriage. He was often away from home on legal or political business. Polk's outstanding record in the legislature brought him opportunities he could not resist. The Jackson supporters, for instance, had big plans for him. They thought he ought to run for the United States Congress.

In the presidential election of 1824, Jackson received more votes than his opponent, John Quincy Adams. But he did not have a majority of all the votes cast. In line with the Constitution, the election was turned over to the House of Representatives. With Henry Clay's leadership, the

President John Quincy Adams

House elected Adams. Jackson's angry followers were determined to make Jackson the next president. Polk decided to run for Congress and work even harder for "Old Hickory," as Jackson was called.

In 1825, Polk was back on his horse, riding constantly throughout a much larger district. The odds were against him. But he was so sincere and so earnest that he persuaded the people to vote for him. In the fall of 1825, the young congressman-elect left his wife behind in their Columbia cottage and set out on horseback again—this time for Washington.

Chapter 4

Jacksonian and Speaker of the House

There was not much to see in Washington in 1825. In dry seasons Pennsylvania Avenue was a cloud of dust, and in winter it was usually knee-deep in mud. After over thirty years of work—hampered when British troops burned it in 1814—the domed Capitol was just nearing completion. Houses and shops were widely scattered over a dreary marshland. Few lawmakers brought their wives and families to live in Washington.

It was common practice for a group of friendly congressmen to organize a "mess" in a boardinghouse or hotel. Each man had a room to himself, where he slept, received visitors, and handled the heavy correspondence of an age before telephones. The men took their meals together at the long dining room table and spent their evening playing cards or talking in the parlor.

Opposite page: James Polk in a formal pose

Secretary of State Henry Clay

Once his living arrangements were settled, Polk was ready for the congressional session that began in December. From the beginning, he opposed President Adams and his secretary of state, Henry Clay. Polk considered them enemies of the people. Adams and Clay wanted high tariffs, which favored the industrial North, and internal improvements—roads, canals, and harbors in certain states—that would be paid for by the federal government.

In a circular dated March 4, 1827, Polk wrote to his constituents in Tennessee that the "present dynasty" wanted to give "the Federal Head all possible power." But the Jacksonians, he went on, upheld Jeffersonian beliefs. They "regard the Constitution as a charter of limited powers." If the Constitution did not specifically grant a certain power to the federal government, it was "reserved to the States and to the people. . . ."

As a congressman, Polk steadfastly maintained his position against Clay's "American System," which called for high land prices as well as high tariffs. Polk was against high land prices because they kept people from going west. This meant that northern manufacturers in the East had plenty of workers and could keep their wages low. At the same time, high tariffs (taxes on goods from other countries) meant higher prices.

High tariffs also produced a surplus of federal monies that Adams and Clay wanted to use for internal improvements. Polk argued that, to continue to support internal improvements, the government would have to tax the people more and more. He would rather lower taxes as much as possible and "bring the government back to what it was intended to be—a plain economical government."

Polk was to be elected to a total of seven terms in Congress. After his first winter away from home, Sarah was determined to accompany him to the capital. Once in Washington, Sarah made sure she was in the ladies' gallery whenever her husband addressed the House. The Polks would spend the next decade living in Washington during congressional sessions and returning to Tennessee for their summers and autumns. (In those days, sessions began in December and usually ended in late spring.)

Polk was one of the new-style congressmen representing the common man. He thought long, pompous speeches were a waste of time. Instead, he spoke in a clear, low-pitched voice and calmly set forth his facts. This baffled people of the old school of orators, including Adams and Clay. But Polk had no desire for their approval.

A campaign parade for Andrew Jackson

Almost immediately after the House elected Adams
president, Andrew Jackson had resigned from the Senate.
He wanted to devote all his efforts to running for president in 1828. Working from the Hermitage in Tennessee,
Jackson came to rely on Polk for inside information about
what was going on in Washington. His campaign would last
for four years and become one of the dirtiest election cam-
paigns in American history.

As a result of Jackson's second bid for the presidency, the nation's one party—Jefferson's Democratic-Republican party—split into two. The Adams-Clay group became the National Republicans, later known as the Whigs. The "Jackson men" eventually became known as the Democrats.

The Adams-Clay people viciously attacked Jackson, trying to weaken his popularity. They described him as an ignorant man who could not read or write and even charged him with being a murderer. Polk took a leading part in defending Jackson and digging up evidence to clear his name.

During this time, Samuel Polk died, and James inherited a major share of his father's large estate. He also became the new head of the family and had to look after his mother and younger brothers and sisters. Most of his brothers had wild streaks that got them into constant trouble, which Polk had to straighten out. His health suffered because of these family problems and the demands of his job as congressman, as well as the strain of campaigning for Jackson.

Despite the ceaseless attacks upon him, Jackson was elected president in 1828 by a wide margin. At his inaugural reception, a wildly enthusiastic crowd trampled mud into the White House, smashed china and glassware, and even knocked waiters off their feet. But Jackson stood tall and dignified on his day of victory.

Polk continued to work for Jackson from his seat in Congress. In 1828, while Adams was still president, Henry Clay and other supporters of high tariffs had successfully passed the "Tariff of Abominations." (Hoping to win support in the northeast, Jackson men had also supported the tariff, as they never expected it to pass!) Polk believed that this tariff unfairly protected the manufacturers of one section of the country at the expense of other sections, particularly the agricultural South.

South Carolina, led by John Calhoun, soon threatened *nullification*—that is, the state threatened that it would refuse to obey the federal tariff laws.

Nullification became a dangerous issue in the beginning of Jackson's term. Polk agreed with Jackson that it was unconstitutional for a state to disobey the laws of the Union while enjoying the privileges of the Union. Jackson proposed a Force Bill that would allow the federal government to use military force against South Carolina if necessary. Polk was among his supporters who passed the bill in Congress, even though he sympathized with the South's position. He believed, with Jackson, that the Union of all the states was more important than any of the individual states' interests.

When the tariff issue reached this crisis, Polk was on the Foreign Affairs Committee. Then he was transferred to the Ways and Means Committee, which was expected to come up with a tariff reform bill. Much of the work fell to Polk in the feverish attempt to resolve the problem before the end of the congressional session. But Clay and Calhoun finally came to an agreement. The resulting Compromise Tariff of 1833 made Polk's efforts at reform unnecessary. Nevertheless, Polk was beginning to be recognized as one of the leading Jacksonians of the House.

Jackson toasting the Union at a banquet during the nullification controversy

James Polk was to play an even greater role in the bitter struggle over the Bank of the United States. Although the federal government deposited its money there, the bank was basically a private, profit-making enterprise with vast financial power. President Jackson was determined to destroy it. He believed it operated for the benefit of the rich few rather than for the people as a whole. Nicholas Biddle, who ran the bank, boasted that he had "more personal authority than any President."

In 1832 Congress voted to renew the bank's charter, but Jackson vetoed it. Then in his second term, Jackson declared the Bank of the United States unconstitutional. He removed the government's deposits and placed them in state banks. This shocked many people, and the Senate passed Henry Clay's resolution to censure Jackson.

Polk drafted a report exposing the bank's abuses and defended Jackson's policy. Three years later, the censure against Jackson would be removed. Polk, made chairman of the Ways and Means Committee, became the president's chief spokesman in the House of Representatives. He had gained Jackson's complete confidence.

In 1834 Polk was defeated in a bid for Speaker of the House. But in December of 1835, after a stormy contest, he was elected to this powerful position. He was the first Speaker to be clearly regarded as a party leader, responsible for pushing a party program through the House.

"Mr. Speaker Polk" had to endure savage personal attacks from his opponents. He was once challenged to a duel, but because he did not believe in dueling, he ignored the challenger's scathing insults.

Above: Jackson explains to Uncle Sam why he is taking U.S. goods to another
"storehouse."   Below: A cartoon entitled "The Downfall of Mother Bank"

It was during Polk's speakership that the "gag rule" passed, pitting the North against the South. This resolution was intended to prevent debate on the subject of slavery. It provided that all petitions to abolish slavery be set aside, without discussion. Congressman and ex-president John Quincy Adams would struggle for eight years to restore the right of petition. But violent disagreement over the slavery issue raised tempers to such a pitch that members came to the House armed with knives. Physical fighting took place on the floor, and Polk had a hard time maintaining order. Yet a press correspondent wrote of him: "I have never seen a man preside over a popular legislative body with more dignity and effect than Mr. Polk. . . . He is scrupulous in his dress and always appears in the chair as if he were at a dinner party."

The speakership also brought with it heavy social responsibilities. The Polks had been living in a boardinghouse and taking their meals with a regular congressional "mess." Now that they had to entertain dignitaries, they moved to Pennsylvania Avenue, where they could have their own parlor and dining room. Polk ordered "a handsome and fashionable" coach to be "built after the latest style," and Sarah became popular for her social gatherings. When the Polks left Washington in 1837, Sarah was sad to think that they might never return.

James Polk retired from Congress to return to Tennessee. Back home he was needed to bolster the Democrats of the state. In 1839 he was elected governor—for only one term—and would have to wait three difficult years for his next important role in American politics.

Opposite page: A portrait of Mrs. Polk

Chapter 5

"Young Hickory"

In May 1844, when the shouting of the Democratic convention died down, the dark-horse candidate had another battle ahead of him. Echoing Henry Clay, the Whigs sneered, "Who is James K. Polk?"

It was not yet thought proper for presidential candidates to make tours or speeches. People would have been shocked if a candidate for the nation's highest office tried to introduce himself and ask for their support. Candidates could write letters to friends expressing their views, which would then be published. They could also work behind the scenes to direct those who were campaigning for them. But they could never appear to be seeking office themselves.

As the Democratic candidate for president, Polk kept in constant touch with political leaders in the various states. Almost all of his communication was by handwritten letters. Polk outlined articles to go into newspapers and pamphlets. He managed his speakers' schedules and even arranged the buying of food for Democratic barbecues.

His opponent, Henry Clay, had many advantages over Polk. He was considered the most talented politician and leader in American history. Clay was known as an eloquent speaker, and at sixty-seven he still possessed charm and a magnetic personality. The Whigs were solidly united behind him.

The Democrats, on the other hand, remained deeply divided. Many were unsure of the little-known and often-defeated Polk. For this reason, a friend of Polk's urged him to be cautious about everything he said and did. He even suggested that Polk avoid "speaking or writing from now until the election." But then, how was Polk to become better known?

The Whigs had another advantage. Most of the well-to-do business people at the time were loyal Whigs. They had more money to spend to promote their candidate and denounce his opponent. Both parties worked overtime to outdo each other with nasty remarks.

The Whigs said that Polk was a mediocre little man who lacked talent and integrity and could not command respect abroad.

The Democrats replied that Clay "may be a more brilliant orator—but we do not want splendid eloquence to conduct the executive department—neither Washington nor Jefferson was an orator. [Mr. Clay] may be a more dashing politician than Mr. Polk—but we do not want any high flying and daring politician, who soars even beyond the Constitution. . . . We want no aspiring 'moon-reaching' president." The idea of reaching the moon in those days was pretty far-fetched.

Above: Polk welcomes Texas (the lady) to the Union
Below: A cartoonist's view of the 1844 presidential election

One of Polk's and Jackson's enemies called Polk "a blighted burr that has fallen from the mane of the warhorse of the Hermitage."

A Polk supporter replied, "Hereafter [James K. Polk] shall be known by the name that we now give him—it is Young Hickory." The crowd that heard this cheered. Andrew Jackson, whose nickname was Old Hickory, could not last forever, said the orator. Young Hickory would take his place and grow to the same great heights.

General Jackson had been a friend of Sarah Polk's father, Major Childress, and had known her for many years. The ailing Jackson wrote to Sarah, "I am now . . . scarcely able to wield my pen, or to see what I write." But, he went on, "I will put you in the White House you can so adorn if it costs me my life!"

Tension mounted as the election drew near. The voting was scheduled for different days in different states, starting in Pennsylvania and Ohio on the first of November. The results, as they came in one by one, would leave both candidates dangling for two weeks.

Finally, at dawn on November 14, Polk was awakened at his home in Columbia by a special messenger. He was informed that he was the president-elect. James Polk shared his excitement with no one but Sarah. He said nothing to his neighbors and friends until the regular mail brought the news to Columbia the next day. He even accepted words of sympathy for his defeat!

The vote was close. Polk's position on Texas—plus his stance on free trade, low tariffs, and the Oregon question—had helped him. So did the large numbers of Irish and German immigrants, whom the Whigs viewed as foreigners who were not equal to American-born citizens. These new Americans voted heavily Democratic.

Congratulations poured in on Polk from all over the country. But a friend warned him that his opponents were very bitter. He advised Polk to "take some thought of where you go & eat & drink for a little while."

After a victory celebration in Nashville, the president-elect spent three days at the Hermitage with Jackson. They discussed the problem of who should be Polk's cabinet members. These various government department heads would be advising him and must be carefully selected. Polk wanted a "united and harmonious set of Cabinet counsellors" who would have the "good of the country . . . at heart." Some Democrats felt that Polk would need a strong cabinet to tell him what to do. But Polk's response was "I intend to be *myself* the President of the U.S." He would control his advisers and not vice versa.

After his visit to the Hermitage, Polk prepared for the journey to Washington. He and Sarah wanted to travel like any other citizens. They did not want any "show or parade." The Polks traveled by steamboat, carriage, and railroad to get from Tennessee to the capital. At times they could not avoid rowdy public demonstrations. When their train finally arrived in Washington, they were shoved through a packed crowd into another carriage and driven to a hotel. There was such a mass of people surrounding the hotel that Polk had to be lifted in through a window. Moments later he appeared on the second-floor balcony to receive the cheers of the crowd.

The new President Polk on his way to the White House

James and Sarah Polk declined an invitation to outgoing President Tyler's farewell ball. But they attended a cabinet dinner at the White House, where congressmen found Sarah to be a graceful and "very superior person" who dressed with taste.

By contrast, Polk's old friends noted that he was thinner than before. Unless he had his coats cut a size too large, they said, "he would be but the merest . . . fraction of a President." No one quite knew what to expect of "the little man from Tennessee."

**Above: James Polk takes the
presidential oath of office**

**Right: George Mifflin Dallas,
Polk's vice-president**

Chapter 6

Manifest Destiny

After Polk's inauguration in March 1845, nine months would pass before Congress convened. The pace during this period should have been slow and relaxed for Polk, as it had been for the presidents before him. But by the 1840s patronage, or the awarding of government jobs, had become a huge problem. There was no civil service system then, and the president could appoint people to thousands of federal offices throughout the states. This brought a swarm of office-seekers to the White House.

"I sincerely wish I had no office to bestow," Polk lamented. He found the constant clamoring for favors a great waste of his time. "And yet," the president wrote, "I do not see how I am to avoid it without being rude or insulting, which it is not my nature to be."

Polk took upon himself all responsibility for every part of the government's operations. No detail was too small to escape his attention. This, plus the pressing issues of his day, took up the president's every waking moment. But Polk felt his time belonged to the nation. He kept a rigid schedule. Rising every day at dawn, he took a short walk and had an early breakfast. Then he worked steadily until dinner at five, and worked again until late at night.

Jackson continued to write to Polk with advice. On June 6, 1845, barely clinging to life, Old Hickory asked for pen and paper. He wanted to write a final letter to the new president. His adopted son urged him to wait until he felt better.

But "tomorrow, said he, I may not be here." Two days later, Andrew Jackson was gone. His death was a great loss to Polk and to the Democratic party.

Polk's feelings for Jackson were deep. But one of Polk's greatest strengths was his ability to keep his feelings from interfering with his goals. He knew what he wanted to do during his presidency even before he entered office. Two of his most important goals were acquiring California and settling a dispute with Great Britain over the Oregon Territory. (Texas had been annexed in the last days of Tyler's administration.)

In wanting to acquire California, Polk was reflecting an idea that was popular in the 1840s. Many Americans believed that the United States had a "Manifest Destiny," that the nation was meant to spread itself across the continent from the Atlantic to the Pacific. Some believed that all of North America and Mexico should be included in this grand scheme as well.

In his inaugural address, Polk pointed out that the American people were already "establishing the blessings of self-government in valleys of which the rivers flow to the Pacific."

He did not yet mention California publicly. But he asserted that the United States had a "clear and unquestionable" title to the Oregon Territory.

The Oregon Territory extended north to Alaska at the 54°40′ latitude. This included not only the present state of Oregon, but also Washington, Idaho, part of Montana, and British Columbia. At one time, four powers had claims to the Oregon Territory—Spain, Great Britain, Russia, and the United States. By 1825, Spain and Russia had given up their claims.

The United States and Great Britain tried to divide the Oregon Territory between themselves, but they could not reach an agreement. The two countries continued to occupy the area jointly. Under the terms of the joint occupation, the Oregon Territory was open to traders and settlers of both countries.

Two years before Polk's election, "Oregon fever" struck the frontier people of Iowa, Missouri, Illinois, and Kentucky. They came together in Independence, Missouri, and organized parties with some hundred wagons each and thousands of cattle. They hired experienced trappers or fur traders to lead them west over two thousand miles of wilderness.

By 1843 there were several thousand settlers in the Willamette Valley in Oregon.

The western states began to demand annexation of the whole of the Oregon Territory up to the 54°40′ parallel. By 1844, western Democrats had succeeded in forcing their platform on the Democratic party. Though Polk ran his presidential campaign with the slogan "Fifty-Four Forty or Fight," he knew that an agreement between Great Britain and the United States could only be reached at the forty-ninth parallel.

Above: Emigrants fording the Platte River on their way to Oregon
Below: Fort Mitchell, a cavalry outpost on the Oregon Trail

Above: An 1846 cartoon depicting the United States' and Great Britain's disagreement over the Oregon Territory

Right: Another cartoon on the British-U.S. fight over the Oregon boundary. The caption has England saying, "What, you young Yankee-Noodle, strike your own father?"

Yet another Oregon controversy cartoon, entitled "Who's Afraid?"

The tide of American settlers flowing into Oregon alarmed the British. And the Democratic campaign for the whole of the Oregon Territory angered them. It was clear when Polk took office that an agreement must be reached soon. A crisis was at hand, and many Americans feared another war with England. This was all the more threatening because the United States was on the verge of war with Mexico over the annexation of Texas. A double war would be disastrous to the nation.

Polk carried the problem to Congress. He recommended that Congress adopt a resolution serving "notice" on the

British that the U.S. wished to terminate the Convention of Joint Occupation. The tone of his message seemed warlike and assured the expansionists that Polk would demand the whole of the Oregon Territory. But in letters to his foreign minister in London, Polk wrote that if the British were to propose that the boundary line be drawn at forty-nine degrees, the United States would be open to discussion. He added, however, that he would not grant free navigation of the Columbia River south of the forty-nine degree line, which the British desired.

While congressmen argued over how much of the Oregon Territory the United States should demand, Polk kept his thoughts and feelings to himself. He proceeded to apply the necessary pressure to Great Britain that would assure a reasonable settlement while avoiding war. And in June 1846, he was able to get a compromise treaty through Congress.

The treaty divided the territory of about half a million square miles almost equally between the two countries. The United States gained Washington, Oregon, and Idaho. Vancouver Island, including the portion south of the forty-ninth parallel, went to Great Britain. This meant that the United States had finally established its permanent northern boundary.

While the Oregon debates were still raging in Congress, the United States' relations with Mexico had been rapidly growing worse. War with England was avoided at the same time that war with Mexico broke out. Polk had been in office a little over a year, and his contribution to Manifest Destiny had only begun.

Chapter 7

War with Mexico

Polk hoped to avoid war with Mexico. During his last days in office, President Tyler had pushed a joint resolution through Congress that offered immediate annexation to Texas. Mexico refused to recognize Texan independence and broke off diplomatic relations with the United States. On the Fourth of July, 1845, Texas accepted the terms of annexation. President Polk ordered General Zachary Taylor to occupy Texas in order to defend it from possible Mexican attack.

In November, Polk sent a newly appointed minister, John Slidell, on a secret mission to Mexico. Slidell was to discuss claims against the Mexican government by American citizens who had been living in Texas. Mexican revolutions had caused them over three million dollars in damages, which Mexico could not afford to pay.

Slidell was also to discuss the boundary dispute between Mexico and the United States. Polk maintained that the boundary was the Rio Grande. Mexico insisted it was the Nueces River, about 150 miles north.

John Slidell, Polk's minister to Mexico

Through Slidell, Polk hoped to settle the Texas boundary and purchase the Mexican province of California. The American government would be willing to pay all claims against Mexico if Mexico would recognize Texas annexation and the Rio Grande boundary. Polk also gave Slidell the power to offer as much as thirty million dollars if Mexico would sell California and all or part of the New Mexico Territory to the United States.

California had begun to worry Polk in the fall of 1845. Mexico's weak hold on the province was slipping, and Mexico was considering selling it to Great Britain. This was most alarming at a time when the United States and Great Britain still had not settled the Oregon question.

In October, Polk sent instructions to the American consul in Monterey, south of San Francisco. Americans (who were foreigners in California) were to support any revolution of its citizens that would lead to independence from Mexico. An independent California could do as Texas had done. California's leaders should be assured that if they wanted to be annexed, they would be welcomed into the Union.

The Whigs were against the idea of Manifest Destiny. They thought national authority should be kept within a limited area.

The Democrats, however, were more likely to agree with Senator James Buchanan when he said, "To talk of confining the American spirit of emigration within limits was like talking of limiting the stars in their courses." But in 1846, when Polk decided that California should be "Americanized," he kept his plans quiet.

Polk wanted to send volunteers to California—skilled craftsmen, farmers, blacksmiths—people who could turn the wilderness into thriving towns and cities. When his plan was revealed, one outraged opponent cried out, "The mask is off." He accused Polk of secretly planning "invasion, conquest, and colonization . . . in a distant region of the globe" that could not possibly be reached in less than four to six months.

In the spring of 1846, Polk also sent John Charles Frémont, an army topographer, on a scientific mission — with sixty-two armed men. Guided by Kit Carson, Frémont's party made its way to California. On the west coast, Commodore John Drake Sloat, commander of the Pacific Squadron of the United States, was instructed to stand ready in the event that the United States and Mexico should go to war.

When the Mexican government refused to meet with Slidell, Polk ordered General Zachary Taylor to the disputed area between the Nueces and the Rio Grande. Taylor's men arrived at the mouth of the Rio Grande on March 28, 1846. Across the 100-yard width of the river they could see the Mexican city of Matamoros. Mexicans climbed onto their roofs to look back at the Americans.

On April 24, a Mexican force crossed the Rio Grande well above its mouth. It met a party of sixty-three American dragoons, or army cavalrymen. When the dragoons found themselves surrounded, they tried to fight their way out. Three were killed, many wounded, and the rest taken prisoner.

Because Mexico had continued to reject Slidell, the American minister advised Polk to declare war against Mexico. Polk was already preparing a message to Congress when word reached him that Americans had been killed by Mexicans.

On May 11, 1845, Polk presented his war message to Congress. "Mexico has invaded our territory," he said (though the territory was in dispute), "and shed American blood upon the American soil."

Above: A pack mule on John Frémont's expedition, overcome by cold and exhaustion
Below: Kit Carson tells tales around the campfire

General Zachary Taylor, hero of the Mexican War, at the Battle of Buena Vista

Polk did not ask Congress to declare war but to recognize that a state of war existed "by the act of Mexico herself." He also asked that Congress provide "the means for prosecuting the war with vigor, and thus hastening the restoration of peace."

Whigs in Congress were against the war with Mexico. But most Americans were for it. One young Whig congressman named Abraham Lincoln dared to speak out against the war. At home, in Illinois, Lincoln was cursed, and he lost his people's support in the next election. Because General Taylor (also a future president) favored the Whigs, his party could not refuse to back him. The House voted 174 to 14, the Senate 40 to 2. The Mexican War was official.

Congressman David Wilmot

In August, Congressman David Wilmot of Pennsylvania brought the question of slavery into the picture. The Wilmot Proviso declared that slavery should not exist in any territory acquired from Mexico as a result of the war. This led to heated debates in Congress about slavery. Polk was dismayed. He insisted that slavery had nothing to do with the war. Though Polk was against slavery, he did not believe it should be a political issue. "The agitation of the slavery question is mischievous and wicked," he declared, "and proceeds from no patriotic motive." The proviso passed the House and was defeated in the Senate. But it succeeded in deepening the split between the pro- and anti-slavery sections of the country.

The defeat of the Mexican army at Buena Vista

Polk had hoped for a quick peace. He hoped the fighting would go on only long enough for the United States to obtain the boundary he had set in his peaceful instructions to Slidell. But the war was to last almost a year and a half. Through General Taylor, Polk sent a message to the Mexican people: "We come to overthrow the tyrants who have destroyed your liberties, but we come to make no war upon the people of Mexico."

In February 1847, Taylor defeated the Mexican army at Buena Vista. General Winfield Scott took Vera Cruz in March and, in September, occupied the capital at Mexico City.

Two artists' versions of General Winfield Scott entering Mexico City

A daguerreotype of Commodore John Drake Sloat

Meanwhile, in California, Frémont had incited American settlers to capture Sonoma, north of San Francisco, and to proclaim the short-lived "Bear Flag Republic." Commodore Sloat seized Monterey and San Francisco, and troops under General Stephen W. Kearny captured Santa Fe in New Mexico and marched west to California. With naval forces led by Commodore Robert F. Stockton, Kearny brought California into American hands. Shortly after, an eighty-gun British warship arrived at Monterey. The British admiral aboard had to report back to England that if Great Britain wanted California, she was too late.

Right: Commodore
Robert F. Stockton

Below: General
Stephen W. Kearny

The Treaty of Guadalupe Hidalgo, which took effect in July 1848, ended the Mexican War. The border between the United States and Mexico was fixed at the Rio Grande, and Mexico gave up all or part of modern California, Nevada, Utah, Wyoming, Colorado, Texas, New Mexico, and Arizona. The United States paid Mexico fifteen million dollars and assumed all claims against Mexico by American citizens. More than 500,000 square miles in the southwest were acquired by the United States, the largest single annexation since the Louisiana Purchase, made by Thomas Jefferson in 1803.

Missouri senator Thomas Hart Benton had written: "It is impossible to conceive of an administration less warlike . . . than that of Mr. Polk." Yet Polk was the first president to assert the right of the chief executive to be—in fact as well as in name—the commander-in-chief of the armed forces. Polk brought the Department of War and the U.S. Navy under his direct control, giving orders down to the finest details.

James Polk considered it his greatest success to have acquired the California ports of San Diego, Monterey, and San Francisco. These, he declared, "will enable the United States to command the already valuable and rapidly increasing commerce of the Pacific." Polk prophesied—correctly—the growth of great cities on these harbors. And he helped set off the California gold rush of 1849 with his glowing account of the "abundance of gold" that had been discovered in the newly acquired territory. After Polk's death, his "secret" American volunteers would become the founding fathers of the Golden State.

Above: An American survey team sent to determine the exact location of the Mexican-U.S. border after the war. Below: Panning for gold in California

Above: Sutter's Mill in California, where gold was discovered in 1848
Below: A cartoon on the amazing abilities of newly patented India rubber to expand and contract. This rubber band—stretching from the Atlantic to the Pacific—would propel gold diggers to California when cut on the Atlantic side.

Above: The U.S. Naval Academy in Annapolis, Maryland, a military post before 1845
Below: The Smithsonian Institution in Washington, D.C., built during Polk's term

Chapter 8

The Hardest-
Working President

Polk once wrote: "No President who performs his duty faithfully and conscientiously can have any leisure."

The president took few breaks from his strict routine. Part of his duty, as he saw it, was to receive anyone who wished to call on him at the White House. This meant almost every citizen who visited Washington, plus various religious and military groups, Sunday school children, and even Indian chiefs. Polk set aside Tuesday and Friday evenings every week for visitors. These informal gatherings sometimes drew as many as two hundred people.

Polk was the first president to keep a tight control over the government. All department heads had to present reports to him on what their employees did every day. One government clerk remarked about the hard-working president: "How he manages to perform so great an a-mount of labor . . . every twenty-four hours, is a mystery."

Opposite page: James Polk in his later years

Sarah Polk, a gracious hostess and faithful presidential secretary

Polk was always a frail person, and his body suffered for his labors. He often exhausted himself to the point of illness. Sarah was the first First Lady to be her husband's personal secretary. She constantly tried to keep him from killing himself with work. It was suggested that she order her carriage and demand that the president come along with her for an occasional drive. "I did so," she replied, "and the carriage waited and waited. . . ."

Though she would not allow card-playing or dancing at the White House, the charming and intelligent First Lady was a popular hostess. Sarah Polk held the first annual Thanksgiving dinner at the White House. She also kept the executive mansion filled with Tennessee nephews and nieces, who brightened the life of the childless president. But she could not slow her husband down or prevent his health from growing worse.

Neither the Oregon crisis nor war with Mexico kept Polk from pursuing his other goals. After Jackson's death in 1845, Democratic unity had completely broken down. Polk had to deal with not only his Whig enemies, but also the Democratic factions in Congress who opposed his policies. Still, President Polk was able to get Congress to pass every leading measure of his administration.

Polk was determined to have a tariff that would be fair to all sections of the country, not just the North. He achieved this with the Walker Tariff of 1846. The Walker Tariff lowered taxes on almost all goods imported from other countries. This increased foreign trade and brought down the prices of products that Americans needed.

Another of Polk's goals was to establish an independent treasury that would allow the government to be its own banker. The Whigs, and others who had supported Nicholas Biddle's Bank of the United States, were bitterly against Polk's plan, but he won out. The treasury bill of 1846 freed the government from private banks. Construction began on the Treasury of the United States, a building with fireproof vaults, and the confusion caused by Jackson's fight with Biddle finally came to an end.

A daguerreotype of the Capitol taken in 1846, when Polk was in office

During Polk's administration, the United States would begin to exercise a world influence. Polk held office during a period of revolution in Ireland, France, Germany, and other parts of Europe. It was a time filled with international problems and European meddling on the American continent. Polk strongly restated the Monroe Doctrine, put forth by President James Monroe in 1823: European countries could not establish any colonies in any part of the North American continent without the United States' consent, and they must not interfere in the affairs of New World nations. To this Polk added that the United States would not permit the sale or transfer of any territory in the New World to a European power.

In the spring of 1848, a group of senators tried to get Polk involved in taking Cuba and bringing it into the United States. Polk refused. Spain owned the island, and he proposed, instead, to buy it. Polk's offer was rejected. But he succeeded in enforcing another important policy: The United States must maintain a neutral position toward already established governments.

Polk also succeeded in gaining a treaty with New Granada (present-day Colombia, South America). The treaty resolved the problem of right-of-way for United States citizens across the Isthmus of Panama by guaranteeing the neutrality of that narrow strip of land between the Atlantic and the Pacific oceans.

Polk was the first of the "modern" presidents to view himself as the representative of all the people. He believed that Congress too often represented only the narrow or special interests. He tried to get members of Congress to see issues as matters of national rather than regional importance. But for all his successes, Polk could not keep the country from tearing itself apart. The North and the South were hopelessly divided on the issue of slavery.

There was much heated debate about whether or not slavery should be extended to the territory won from Mexico. Polk was afraid that California might become an independent nation if it did not soon become a state. Up to the last minute of his term in office, he urged Congress to pass a California statehood bill. But the debates continued. Polk would not live to see California admitted to the Union, although in addition to Texas, Iowa and Wisconsin became states during his administration.

Before he even took office, Polk had announced his intention to retire after one term. On the last day of his presidency, he confided to his diary: "I feel exceedingly relieved that I am now free from all public cares. I am sure I shall be a happier man in my retirement than I have been during the four years I have filled the highest office in the gift of my countrymen."

When Polk left office, the United States was half again as large as it had been when he became president. In that brief period, he had acquired all the territory that would complete the first forty-eight states. But Polk would never set foot upon the territories he acquired.

Following the inauguration of his successor, General Zachary Taylor, Polk left Washington for a month-long tour of the South. He was greeted everywhere by cheering crowds and sometimes spent hours shaking hands. At times he was almost overcome by the heat as he rode through the crowded streets or attended dinners he was too ill to enjoy. In Georgia, a sudden thunderstorm frightened his carriage horses. Although they were stopped without accident, Polk was badly shaken. He became so exhausted by the many receptions and banquets given in his honor that he collapsed in New Orleans, Louisiana. He was taken home to Tennessee as quickly as possible, but it would be grueling days before he got there.

Polk had recently purchased the Nashville home of the late Felix Grundy. He called it Polk Place and looked forward to retiring there with Sarah. But he spent his final weeks sorting his papers and overseeing the remodeling of the estate he would never enjoy. Polk grew weaker and

James Buchanan

weaker, and he quietly passed away on June 15, 1849, three months after leaving office. He had been the youngest of the presidents thus far and was the first president whose mother outlived him.

James Buchanan, Polk's secretary of state and a future president, described the change that had come over Polk: "In a brief period of four years [he] had assumed the appearance of an old man." Polk was, said Buchanan, the hardest-working man he had ever known.

The elderly Mrs. Polk (seated) and her "adopted" daughter

Polk was buried in the garden at Polk Place. He left the bulk of his estate to Sarah and requested that their slaves be freed upon her death. But Sarah lived well past the Civil War. She was a widow for forty-two years. During the war she declared Polk Place neutral ground and was treated respectfully by both sides.

Who was James K. Polk? What would Polk's place be in history?

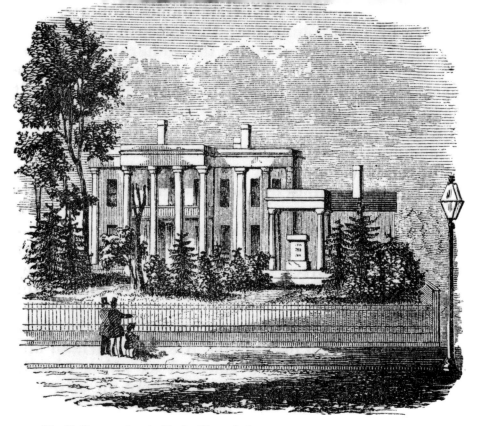

The Polk mansion in Nashville and the monument marking Polk's grave

The people knew who Polk was. He was "Young Hickory." He was their champion. He had grown up on the Tennessee frontier and, as eleventh president, had expanded America's frontiers clear to the Pacific coast. A New York newspaper praised Polk at his passing: "No man and no administration was ever more assailed, and none ever achieved more."

Polk would prove to be the only strong president between Andrew Jackson and Abraham Lincoln. But Whig attitudes prevailed for years, and Polk was either condemned or dismissed as an unimportant figure. It was almost a century after his death before historians realized that James Knox Polk was one of the nation's great presidents.

Chronology of American History

(Shaded area covers events in James K. Polk's lifetime.)

About A.D. 982—Eric the Red, born in Norway, reaches Greenland in one of the first European voyages to North America.

About 985—Eric the Red brings settlers from Iceland to Greenland.

About 1000—Leif Ericson (Eric the Red's son) leads what is thought to be the first European expedition to mainland North America; Leif probably lands in Canada.

1492—Christopher Columbus, seeking a sea route from Spain to the Far East, discovers the New World.

1497—John Cabot reaches Canada in the first English voyage to North America.

1513—Ponce de Léon explores Florida in search of the fabled Fountain of Youth.

1519-1521—Hernando Cortés of Spain conquers Mexico.

1534—French explorers led by Jacques Cartier enter the Gulf of St. Lawrence in Canada.

1540—Spanish explorer Francisco Coronado begins exploring the American Southwest, seeking the riches of the mythical Seven Cities of Cibola.

1565—St. Augustine, Florida, the first permanent European town in what is now the United States, is founded by the Spanish.

1607—Jamestown, Virginia, is founded, the first permanent English town in the present-day U.S.

1608—Frenchman Samuel de Champlain founds the village of Quebec, Canada.

1609—Henry Hudson explores the eastern coast of present-day U.S. for the Netherlands; the Dutch then claim parts of New York, New Jersey, Delaware, and Connecticut and name the area New Netherland.

1619—The English colonies' first shipment of black slaves arrives in Jamestown.

1620—English Pilgrims found Massachusetts' first permanent town at Plymouth.

1621—Massachusetts Pilgrims and Indians hold the famous first Thanksgiving feast in colonial America.

1623—Colonization of New Hampshire is begun by the English.

1624—Colonization of present-day New York State is begun by the Dutch at Fort Orange (Albany).

1625—The Dutch start building New Amsterdam (now New York City).

1630—The town of Boston, Massachusetts, is founded by the English Puritans.

1633—Colonization of Connecticut is begun by the English.

1634—Colonization of Maryland is begun by the English.

1636—Harvard, the colonies' first college, is founded in Massachusetts. Rhode Island colonization begins when Englishman Roger Williams founds Providence.

1638—Delaware colonization begins when Swedish people build Fort Christina at present-day Wilmington.

1640—Stephen Daye of Cambridge, Massachusetts prints *The Bay Psalm Book*, the first English-language book published in what is now the U.S.

1643—Swedish settlers begin colonizing Pennsylvania.

About 1650—North Carolina is colonized by Virginia settlers.

1660—New Jersey colonization is begun by the Dutch at present-day Jersey City.

1670—South Carolina colonization is begun by the English near Charleston.

1673—Jacques Marquette and Louis Jolliet explore the upper Mississippi River for France.

1682—Philadelphia, Pennsylvania, is settled. La Salle explores Mississippi River all the way to its mouth in Louisiana and claims the whole Mississippi Valley for France.

1693—College of William and Mary is founded in Williamsburg, Virginia.

1700—Colonial population is about 250,000.

1703—Benjamin Franklin is born in Boston.

1732—George Washington, first president of the U.S., is born in Westmoreland County, Virginia.

1733—James Oglethorpe founds Savannah, Georgia; Georgia is established as the thirteenth colony.

1735—John Adams, second president of the U.S., is born in Braintree, Massachusetts.

1737—William Byrd founds Richmond, Virginia.

1738—British troops are sent to Georgia over border dispute with Spain.

1739—Black insurrection takes place in South Carolina.

1740—English Parliament passes act allowing naturalization of immigrants to American colonies after seven-year residence.

1743—Thomas Jefferson, third president of the U.S., is born in Albemarle County, Virginia. Benjamin Franklin retires at age thirty-seven to devote himself to scientific inquiries and public service.

1744—King George's War begins; France joins war effort against England.

1745—During King George's War, France raids settlements in Maine and New York.

1747—Classes begin at Princeton College in New Jersey.

1748—The Treaty of Aix-la-Chapelle concludes King George's War.

1749—Parliament legally recognizes slavery in colonies and the inauguration of the plantation system in the South. George Washington becomes the surveyor for Culpepper County in Virginia.

1750—Thomas Walker passes through and names Cumberland Gap on his way toward Kentucky region. Colonial population is about 1,200,000.

1751—James Madison, fourth president of the U.S., is born in Port Conway, Virginia. English Parliament passes Currency Act, banning New England colonies from issuing paper money. George Washington travels to Barbados.

1752—Pennsylvania Hospital, the first general hospital in the colonies, is founded in Philadelphia. Benjamin Franklin uses a kite in a thunderstorm to demonstrate that lightning is a form of electricity.

1753—George Washington delivers command from Virginia Lieutenant Governor Dinwiddie that the French withdraw from the Ohio River Valley; French disregard the demand. Colonial population is about 1,328,000.

1754—French and Indian War begins (extends to Europe as the Seven Years' War). Washington surrenders at Fort Necessity.

1755—French and Indians ambush General Braddock. Washington becomes commander of Virginia troops.

1756—England declares war on France.

1758—James Monroe, fifth president of the U.S., is born in Westmoreland County, Virginia.

1759—Cherokee Indian war begins in southern colonies; hostilities extend to 1761. George Washington marries Martha Dandridge Custis.

1760—George III becomes king of England. Colonial population is about 1,600,000.

1762—England declares war on Spain.

1763—Treaty of Paris concludes the French and Indian War and the Seven Years' War. England gains Canada and most other French lands east of the Mississippi River.

1764—British pass the Sugar Act to gain tax money from the colonists. The issue of taxation without representation is first introduced in Boston. John Adams marries Abigail Smith.

1765—Stamp Act goes into effect in the colonies. Business virtually stops as almost all colonists refuse to use the stamps.

1766—British repeal the Stamp Act.

1767—John Quincy Adams, sixth president of the U.S. and son of second president John Adams, is born in Braintree, Massachusetts. Andrew Jackson, seventh president of the U.S., is born in Waxhaw settlement, South Carolina.

1769—Daniel Boone sights the Kentucky Territory.

1770—In the Boston Massacre, British soldiers kill five colonists and injure six. Townshend Acts are repealed, thus eliminating all duties on imports to the colonies except tea.

1771—Benjamin Franklin begins his autobiography, a work that he will never complete. The North Carolina assembly passes the "Bloody Act," which makes rioters guilty of treason.

1772—Samuel Adams rouses colonists to consider British threats to self-government. Thomas Jefferson marries Martha Wayles Skelton.

1773—English Parliament passes the Tea Act. Colonists dressed as Mohawk Indians board British tea ships and toss 342 casks of tea into the water in what becomes known as the Boston Tea Party. William Henry Harrison is born in Charles City County, Virginia.

1774—British close the port of Boston to punish the city for the Boston Tea Party. First Continental Congress convenes in Philadelphia.

1775—American Revolution begins with battles of Lexington and Concord, Massachusetts. Second Continental Congress opens in Philadelphia. George Washington becomes commander-in-chief of the Continental army.

1776—Declaration of Independence is adopted on July 4.

1777—Congress adopts the American flag with thirteen stars and thirteen stripes. John Adams is sent to France to negotiate peace treaty.

1778—France declares war against Great Britain and becomes U.S. ally.

1779—British surrender to Americans at Vincennes. Thomas Jefferson is elected governor of Virginia. James Madison is elected to the Continental Congress.

1780—Benedict Arnold, first American traitor, defects to the British.

1781—Articles of Confederation go into effect. Cornwallis surrenders to George Washington at Yorktown, ending the American Revolution.

1782—American commissioners, including John Adams, sign peace treaty with British in Paris. Thomas Jefferson's wife, Martha, dies. Martin Van Buren is born in Kinderhook, New York.

1784—Zachary Taylor is born near Barboursville, Virginia.

1785—Congress adopts the dollar as the unit of currency. John Adams is made minister to Great Britain. Thomas Jefferson is appointed minister to France.

1786—Shays' Rebellion begins in Massachusetts.

1787—Constitutional Convention assembles in Philadelphia, with George Washington presiding; U.S. Constitution is adopted. Delaware, New Jersey, and Pennsylvania become states.

1788—Virginia, South Carolina, New York, Connecticut, New Hampshire, Maryland, and Massachusetts become states. U.S. Constitution is ratified. New York City is declared U.S. capital.

1789—Presidential electors elect George Washington and John Adams as first president and vice-president. Thomas Jefferson is appointed secretary of state. North Carolina becomes a state. French Revolution begins.

1790—Supreme Court meets for the first time. Rhode Island becomes a state. First national census in the U.S. counts 3,929,214 persons. John Tyler is born in Charles City County, Virginia.

1791—Vermont enters the Union. U.S. Bill of Rights, the first ten amendments to the Constitution, goes into effect. District of Columbia is established.

1792—Thomas Paine publishes *The Rights of Man*. Kentucky becomes a state. Two political parties are formed in the U.S., Federalist and Republican. Washington is elected to a second term, with Adams as vice-president.

1793—War between France and Britain begins; U.S. declares neutrality. Eli Whitney invents the cotton gin; cotton production and slave labor increase in the South.

1794—Eleventh Amendment to the Constitution is passed, limiting federal courts' power. "Whiskey Rebellion" in Pennsylvania protests federal whiskey tax. James Madison marries Dolley Payne Todd.

1795—George Washington signs the Jay Treaty with Great Britain. Treaty of San Lorenzo, between U.S. and Spain, settles Florida boundary and gives U.S. right to navigate the Mississippi. James Polk is born near Pineville, North Carolina.

1796—Tennessee enters the Union. Washington gives his Farewell Address, refusing a third presidential term. John Adams is elected president and Thomas Jefferson vice-president.

1797—Adams recommends defense measures against possible war with France. Napoleon Bonaparte and his army march against Austrians in Italy. U.S. population is about 4,900,000.

1798—Washington is named commander-in-chief of the U.S. army. Department of the Navy is created. Alien and Sedition Acts are passed. Napoleon's troops invade Egypt and Switzerland.

1799—George Washington dies at Mount Vernon. James Monroe is elected governor of Virginia. French Revolution ends. Napoleon becomes ruler of France.

1800—Thomas Jefferson and Aaron Burr tie for president. U.S. capital is moved from Philadelphia to Washington, D.C. The White House is built as presidents' home. Spain returns Louisiana to France. Millard Fillmore is born in Locke, New York.

1801—After thirty-six ballots, House of Representatives elects Thomas Jefferson president, making Burr vice-president. James Madison is named secretary of state.

1802—Congress abolishes excise taxes. U.S. Military Academy is founded at West Point, New York.

1803—Ohio enters the Union. Louisiana Purchase treaty is signed with France, greatly expanding U.S. territory.

1804—Twelfth Amendment to the Constitution rules that president and vice-president be elected separately. Alexander Hamilton is killed by Vice-President Aaron Burr in a duel. Orleans Territory is established. Napoleon crowns himself emperor of France.

1805—Thomas Jefferson begins his second term as president. Lewis and Clark expedition reaches the Pacific Ocean.

1806—Coinage of silver dollars is stopped; resumes in 1836.

1807—Aaron Burr is acquitted in treason trial. Embargo Act closes U.S. ports to trade.

1808—James Madison is elected president. Congress outlaws importing slaves from Africa.

1810—U.S. population is 7,240,000.

1811—William Henry Harrison defeats Indians at Tippecanoe. Monroe is named secretary of state.

1812—Louisiana becomes a state. U.S. declares war on Britain (War of 1812). James Madison is reelected president. Napoleon invades Russia.

1813—British forces take Fort Niagara and Buffalo, New York.

1814—Francis Scott Key writes "The Star-Spangled Banner." British troops burn much of Washington, D.C., including the White House. Treaty of Ghent ends War of 1812. James Monroe becomes secretary of war.

1815—Napoleon meets his final defeat at Battle of Waterloo.

1816—James Monroe is elected president. Indiana becomes a state.

1817—Mississippi becomes a state. Construction on Erie Canal begins.

1818—Illinois enters the Union. The present thirteen-stripe flag is adopted. Border between U.S. and Canada is agreed upon.

1819—Alabama becomes a state. U.S. purchases Florida from Spain. Thomas Jefferson establishes the University of Virginia.

1820—James Monroe is reelected. In the Missouri Compromise, Maine enters the Union as a free (non-slave) state.

1821—Missouri enters the Union as a slave state. Santa Fe Trail opens the American Southwest. Mexico declares independence from Spain. Napoleon Bonaparte dies.

1822—U.S. recognizes Mexico and Colombia. Liberia in Africa is founded as a home for freed slaves.

1823—Monroe Doctrine closes North and South America to European colonizing or invasion.

1824—House of Representatives elects John Quincy Adams president when none of the four candidates wins a majority in national election. Mexico becomes a republic.

1825—Erie Canal is opened. U.S. population is 11,300,000.

1826—Thomas Jefferson and John Adams both die on July 4, the fiftieth anniversary of the Declaration of Independence.

1828—Andrew Jackson is elected president. Tariff of Abominations is passed, cutting imports.

1829—James Madison attends Virginia's constitutional convention. Slavery is abolished in Mexico.

1830—Indian Removal Act to resettle Indians west of the Mississippi is approved.

1831—James Monroe dies in New York City. James A. Garfield is born in Orange, Ohio. Cyrus McCormick develops his reaper.

1832—Andrew Jackson, nominated by the new Democratic Party, is reelected president.

1833—Britain abolishes slavery in its colonies.

1835—Federal government becomes debt-free for the first time.

1836—Martin Van Buren becomes president. Texas wins independence from Mexico. Arkansas joins the Union. James Madison dies at Montpelier, Virginia.

1837—Michigan enters the Union. U.S. population is 15,900,000.

1840—William Henry Harrison is elected president.

1841—President Harrison dies in Washington, D.C., one month after inauguration. Vice-President John Tyler succeeds him.

1844—James Knox Polk is elected president. Samuel Morse sends first telegraphic message.

1845—Texas and Florida become states. Potato famine in Ireland causes massive emigration from Ireland to U.S. Andrew Jackson dies near Nashville, Tennessee.

1846—Iowa enters the Union. War with Mexico begins.

1847—U.S. captures Mexico City.

1848—Zachary Taylor becomes president. Treaty of Guadalupe Hidalgo ends Mexico-U.S. war. Wisconsin becomes a state.

1849—James Polk dies in Nashville, Tennessee.

1850—President Taylor dies in Washington, D.C.; Vice-President Millard Fillmore succeeds him. California enters the Union, breaking tie between slave and free states.

1852—Franklin Pierce is elected president.

1853—Gadsden Purchase transfers Mexican territory to U.S.

1854—"War for Bleeding Kansas" is fought between slave and free states.

1855—Czar Nicholas I of Russia dies, succeeded by Alexander II.

1856—James Buchanan is elected president. In Massacre of Potawatomi Creek, Kansas-slavers are murdered by free-staters.

1858—Minnesota enters the Union. Theodore Roosevelt is born in New York City.

1859—Oregon becomes a state.

1860—Abraham Lincoln is elected president; South Carolina secedes from the Union in protest.

1861—Arkansas, Tennessee, North Carolina, and Virginia secede. Kansas enters the Union as a free state. Civil War begins.

1862—Union forces capture Fort Henry, Roanoke Island, Fort Donelson, Jacksonville, and New Orleans; Union armies are defeated at the battles of Bull Run and Fredericksburg. Martin Van Buren dies in Kinderhook, New York. John Tyler dies near Charles City, Virginia.

1863—Lincoln issues Emancipation Proclamation; all slaves held in rebelling territories are declared free. West Virginia becomes a state.

1864—Abraham Lincoln is reelected. Nevada becomes a state.

1865—Lincoln is assassinated, succeeded by Andrew Johnson. U.S. Civil War ends on May 26. Thirteenth Amendment abolishes slavery.

1867—Nebraska becomes a state. U.S. buys Alaska from Russia for $7,200,000. Reconstruction Acts are passed.

1868—President Johnson is impeached for violating Tenure of Office Act, but is acquitted by Senate. Ulysses S. Grant is elected president. Fourteenth Amendment prohibits voting discrimination.

1870—Fifteenth Amendment gives blacks the right to vote.

1872—Grant is reelected over Horace Greeley. General Amnesty Act pardons ex-Confederates.

1874—Millard Fillmore dies in Buffalo, New York. Herbert Hoover is born in West Branch, Iowa.

1876—Colorado enters the Union. "Custer's last stand": he and his men are massacred by Sioux Indians at Little Big Horn, Montana.

1877—Rutherford B. Hayes is elected president as all disputed votes are awarded to him.

1880—James A. Garfield is elected president.

1881—President Garfield is assassinated and dies in Elberon, New Jersey. Vice-President Chester A. Arthur succeeds him.

1882—U.S. bans Chinese immigration. Franklin D. Roosevelt is born in Hyde Park, New York.

1886—Statue of Liberty is dedicated.

1888—Benjamin Harrison is elected president.

1889—North Dakota, South Dakota, Washington, and Montana become states.

1890—Dwight D. Eisenhower is born in Denison, Texas. Idaho and Wyoming become states.

1892—Grover Cleveland is elected president.

1896—William McKinley is elected president. Utah becomes a state.

1898—U.S. declares war on Spain over Cuba.

1899—Philippines demand independence from U.S.

1900—McKinley is reelected. Boxer Rebellion against foreigners in China begins.

1901—McKinley is assassinated by anarchist; he is succeeded by Theodore Roosevelt.

1902—U.S. acquires perpetual control over Panama Canal.

1903—Alaskan frontier is settled.

1904—Russian-Japanese War breaks out. Theodore Roosevelt wins presidential election.

1905—Treaty of Portsmouth signed, ending Russian-Japanese War.

1906—U.S. troops occupy Cuba.

1907—President Roosevelt bars all Japanese immigration. Oklahoma enters the Union.

1908—William Howard Taft becomes president. Lyndon B. Johnson is born near Stonewall, Texas.

1909 — NAACP is founded under W.E.B. DuBois

1910 — China abolishes slavery.

1911 — Chinese Revolution begins.

1912 — Woodrow Wilson is elected president. Arizona and New Mexico become states.

1913 — Federal income tax is introduced in U.S. through the Sixteenth Amendment. Richard Nixon is born in Yorba Linda, California.

1914 — World War I begins.

1915 — British liner *Lusitania* is sunk by German submarine.

1916 — Wilson is reelected president.

1917 — U.S. breaks diplomatic relations with Germany. Czar Nicholas of Russia abdicates as revolution begins. U.S. declares war on Austria-Hungary. John F. Kennedy is born in Brookline, Massachusetts.

1918 — Wilson proclaims "Fourteen Points" as war aims. On November 11, armistice is signed between Allies and Germany.

1919 — Eighteenth Amendment prohibits sale and manufacture of intoxicating liquors. Wilson presides over first League of Nations; wins Nobel Peace Prize. Theodore Roosevelt dies in Oyster Bay, New York.

1920 — Nineteenth Amendment (women's suffrage) is passed. Warren Harding is elected president.

1921 — Adolf Hitler's stormtroopers begin to terrorize political opponents.

1922 — Irish Free State is established. Soviet states form USSR. Benito Mussolini forms Fascist government in Italy.

1923 — President Harding dies; he is succeeded by Vice-President Calvin Coolidge.

1924 — Coolidge is elected president.

1925 — Hitler reorganizes Nazi Party and publishes first volume of *Mein Kampf.*

1926 — Fascist youth organizations founded in Germany and Italy. Republic of Lebanon proclaimed.

1927 — Stalin becomes Soviet dictator. Economic conference in Geneva attended by fifty-two nations.

1928 — Herbert Hoover is elected president. U.S. and many other nations sign Kellogg-Briand pacts to outlaw war.

1929 — Stock prices in New York crash on "Black Thursday"; the Great Depression begins.

1930 — Bank of U.S. and its many branches close (most significant bank failure of the year).

1931 — Emigration from U.S. exceeds immigration for first time as Depression deepens.

1932 — Franklin D. Roosevelt wins presidential election in a Democratic landslide.

1933 — First concentration camps are erected in Germany. U.S. recognizes USSR and resumes trade. Twenty-First Amendment repeals prohibition.

1934 — Severe dust storms hit Plains states. President Roosevelt passes U.S. Social Security Act.

1936 — Roosevelt is reelected. Spanish Civil War begins. Hitler and Mussolini form Rome-Berlin Axis.

1937 — Roosevelt signs Neutrality Act.

1938 — Roosevelt sends appeal to Hitler and Mussolini to settle European problems amicably.

1939 — Germany takes over Czechoslovakia and invades Poland, starting World War II.

1940 — Roosevelt is reelected for a third term.

1941 — Japan bombs Pearl Harbor. U.S. declares war on Japan. Germany and Italy declare war on U.S.; U.S. then declares war on them.

1942 — Allies agree not to make separate peace treaties with the enemies. U.S. government transfers more than 100,000 Nisei (Japanese-Americans) from west coast to inland concentration camps.

1943—Allied bombings of Germany begin.

1944—Roosevelt is reelected for a fourth term. Allied forces invade Normandy on D-Day.

1945—President Franklin D. Roosevelt dies in Warm Springs, Georgia; Vice-President Harry S. Truman succeeds him. Mussolini is killed; Hitler commits suicide. Germany surrenders. U.S. drops atomic bomb on Hiroshima; Japan surrenders; end of World War II.

1946—U.N. General Assembly holds its first session in London. Peace conference of twenty-one nations is held in Paris.

1947—Peace treaties are signed in Paris. "Cold War" is in full swing.

1948—U.S. passes Marshall Plan Act, providing $17 billion in aid for Europe. U.S. recognizes new nation of Israel. India and Pakistan become free of British rule. Truman is elected president.

1949—Republic of Eire is proclaimed in Dublin. Russia blocks land route access from Western Germany to Berlin; airlift begins. U.S., France, and Britain agree to merge their zones of occupation in West Germany. Apartheid program begins in South Africa.

1950—Riots in Johannesburg, South Africa, against apartheid. North Korea invades South Korea. U.N. forces land in South Korea and recapture Seoul.

1951—Twenty-Second Amendment limits president to two terms.

1952—Dwight D. Eisenhower resigns as supreme commander in Europe and is elected president.

1953—Stalin dies; struggle for power in Russia follows. Rosenbergs are executed for espionage.

1954—U.S. and Japan sign mutual defense agreement.

1955—Blacks in Montgomery, Alabama, boycott segregated bus lines.

1956—Eisenhower is reelected president. Soviet troops march into Hungary.

1957—U.S. agrees to withdraw ground forces from Japan. Russia launches first satellite, *Sputnik.*

1958—European Common Market comes into being. Alaska becomes the forty-ninth state. Fidel Castro begins war against Batista government in Cuba.

1959—Hawaii becomes fiftieth state. Castro becomes premier of Cuba. De Gaulle is proclaimed president of the Fifth Republic of France.

1960—Historic debates between Senator John F. Kennedy and Vice-President Richard Nixon are televised. Kennedy is elected president. Brezhnev becomes president of USSR.

1961—Berlin Wall is constructed. Kennedy and Khrushchev confer in Vienna. In Bay of Pigs incident, Cubans trained by CIA attempt to overthrow Castro.

1962—U.S. military council is established in South Vietnam.

1963—Riots and beatings by police and whites mark civil rights demonstrations in Birmingham, Alabama; 30,000 troops are called out. Martin Luther King, Jr., is arrested. Freedom marchers descend on Washington, D.C., to demonstrate. President Kennedy is assassinated in Dallas, Texas; Vice-President Lyndon B. Johnson is sworn in as president.

1964—U.S. aircraft bomb North Vietnam. Johnson is elected president. Herbert Hoover dies in New York City.

1965—U.S. combat troops arrive in South Vietnam.

1966—Thousands protest U.S. policy in Vietnam. National Guard quells race riots in Chicago.

1967—Six-Day War between Israel and Arab nations.

1968—Martin Luther King, Jr., is assassinated in Memphis, Tennessee. Senator Robert Kennedy is assassinated in Los Angeles. Riots and police brutality take place at Democratic National Convention in Chicago. Richard Nixon is elected president. Czechoslovakia is invaded by Soviet troops.

1969—Dwight D. Eisenhower dies in Washington, D.C. Hundreds of thousands of people in several U.S. cities demonstrate against Vietnam War.

1970—Four Vietnam War protesters are killed by National Guardsmen at Kent State University in Ohio.

1971—Twenty-Sixth Amendment allows eighteen-year-olds to vote.

1972—Nixon visits Communist China; is reelected president in near-record landslide. Watergate affair begins when five men are arrested in the Watergate hotel complex in Washington, D.C. Nixon announces resignations of aides Haldeman, Ehrlichman, and Dean and Attorney General Kleindienst as a result of Watergate-related charges. Harry S. Truman dies in Kansas City, Missouri.

1973—Vice-President Spiro Agnew resigns; Gerald Ford is named vice-president. Vietnam peace treaty is formally approved after nineteen months of negotiations. Lyndon B. Johnson dies in San Antonio, Texas.

1974—As a result of Watergate cover-up, impeachment is considered; Nixon resigns and Ford becomes president. Ford pardons Nixon and grants limited amnesty to Vietnam War draft evaders and military deserters.

1975—U.S. civilians are evacuated from Saigon, South Vietnam, as Communist forces complete takeover of South Vietnam.

1976—U.S. celebrates its Bicentennial. James Earl Carter becomes president.

1977—Carter pardons most Vietnam draft evaders, numbering some 10,000.

1980—Ronald Reagan is elected president.

1981—President Reagan is shot in the chest in assassination attempt. Sandra Day O'Connor is appointed first woman justice of the Supreme Court.

1983—U.S. troops invade island of Grenada.

1984—Reagan is reelected president. Democratic candidate Walter Mondale's running mate, Geraldine Ferraro, is the first woman selected for vice-president by a major U.S. political party.

1985—Soviet Communist Party secretary Konstantin Chernenko dies; Mikhail Gorbachev succeeds him. U.S. and Soviet officials discuss arms control in Geneva. Reagan and Gorbachev hold summit conference in Geneva. Racial tensions accelerate in South Africa.

1986—Space shuttle *Challenger* explodes shortly after takeoff; crew of seven dies. U.S. bombs bases in Libya. Corazon Aquino defeats Ferdinand Marcos in Philippine presidential election.

1987—Iraqi missile rips the U.S. frigate *Stark* in the Persian Gulf, killing thirty-seven American sailors. Congress holds hearings to investigate sale of U.S. arms to Iran to finance Nicaraguan *contra* movement.

1988—George Bush is elected president. President Reagan and Soviet leader Gorbachev sign INF treaty, eliminating intermediate nuclear forces. Severe drought sweeps the United States.

Index

Page numbers in boldface type indicate illustrations.

About the Author

Dee Lillegard is the author of *September To September*, *Poems for All Year Round*, a teacher resource, and many easy readers, including titles for Childrens Press's *I Can Be* career series. For the *Encyclopedia of Presidents* series, she has written biographies of John Tyler, James K. Polk, James A. Garfield, and Richard Nixon. Over two hundred of Ms. Lillegard's stories, poems, and puzzles have appeared in numerous children's magazines. Ms. Lillegard lives in the San Francisco Bay Area, where she teaches Writing for Children.